It's about Time

Minutes

by Kimberly M. Hutmacher

Gail Saunders-Smith, PhD,
Consulting Editor

CAPSTONE PRESS
a capstone imprint

Pebble Books are published by Capstone Press,
1710 Roe Crest Drive, North Mankato, Minnesota 56003
www.capstonepub.com

Copyright © 2013 by Capstone Press, a Capstone imprint. All rights reserved.
No part of this publication may be reproduced in whole or in part, or stored in a retrieval system, or transmitted in any form or by any means, electronic, mechanical, photocopying, recording, or otherwise, without written permission of the publisher.
For information regarding permission, write to Capstone Press,
1710 Roe Crest Drive, North Mankato, Minnesota 56003.

Library of Congress Cataloging-in-Publication Data
Hutmacher, Kimberly.
Minutes / by Kimberly M. Hutmacher.
p. cm. — (Pebble books. It's about time)
Summary: "Simple rhyming text and color photographs present minutes as a unit of time"— Provided by publisher.
Includes bibliographical references and index.
ISBN 978-1-4296-8576-4 (library binding)
ISBN 978-1-4296-9352-3 (paperback)
ISBN 978-1-62065-284-8 (ebook PDF)
1. Time—Juvenile literature. 2. Time measurements—Juvenile literature. 3. Clocks and watches—Juvenile literature. I. Title.
QB209.5.H885 2013
529'.2—dc23 2012004669

Note to Parents and Teachers

The It's about Time set supports national mathematics standards related to measurement and data. This book describes and illustrates minutes. The images support early readers in understanding the text. The repetition of words and phrases helps early readers learn new words. This book also introduces early readers to subject-specific vocabulary words, which are defined in the Glossary section. Early readers may need assistance to read some words and to use the Table of Contents, Glossary, Read More, Internet Sites, and Index sections of the book.

Printed in the United States of America in North Mankato, Minnesota.
042012 006682CGF12

Table of Contents

LER 2094
12
1
2
3
4
5
6
7
8
9
10
11
5
10
20
25
30
35
40
45
55
60

What Is a Minute?

What is a minute?

It's a length of time.

Let's look at minutes

with a simple rhyme.

Telling Time with Minutes

Clocks mark the time.

They are such useful tools.

They measure every minute—

help us be on time for school.

hour hand
second hand
minute hand
one minute

An analog clock has no eyes,
just three hands and a face.
The minute hand gets 60 seconds
to go to its next place.

SHARP Carousel
minutes
10:05
QTY
LB
OZ
SIZE
CUPS
colon

Digital clocks have no hands.
Only numbers in a line.
Minutes come after the colon.
Now we can tell the time!

How Long Is a Minute?

A minute passes by you when ...

You roast a marshmallow.

Button your coat.

Play tic-tac-toe

or jot a note.

Fold a plane.

Comb your hair.

Take a turn

at show and share.

HAPPY

Unwrap a gift.

Climb and slide.

Practice math.

Seek or hide!

Top a sundae.

Fill a balloon.

Bait a hook.

Sing a tune!

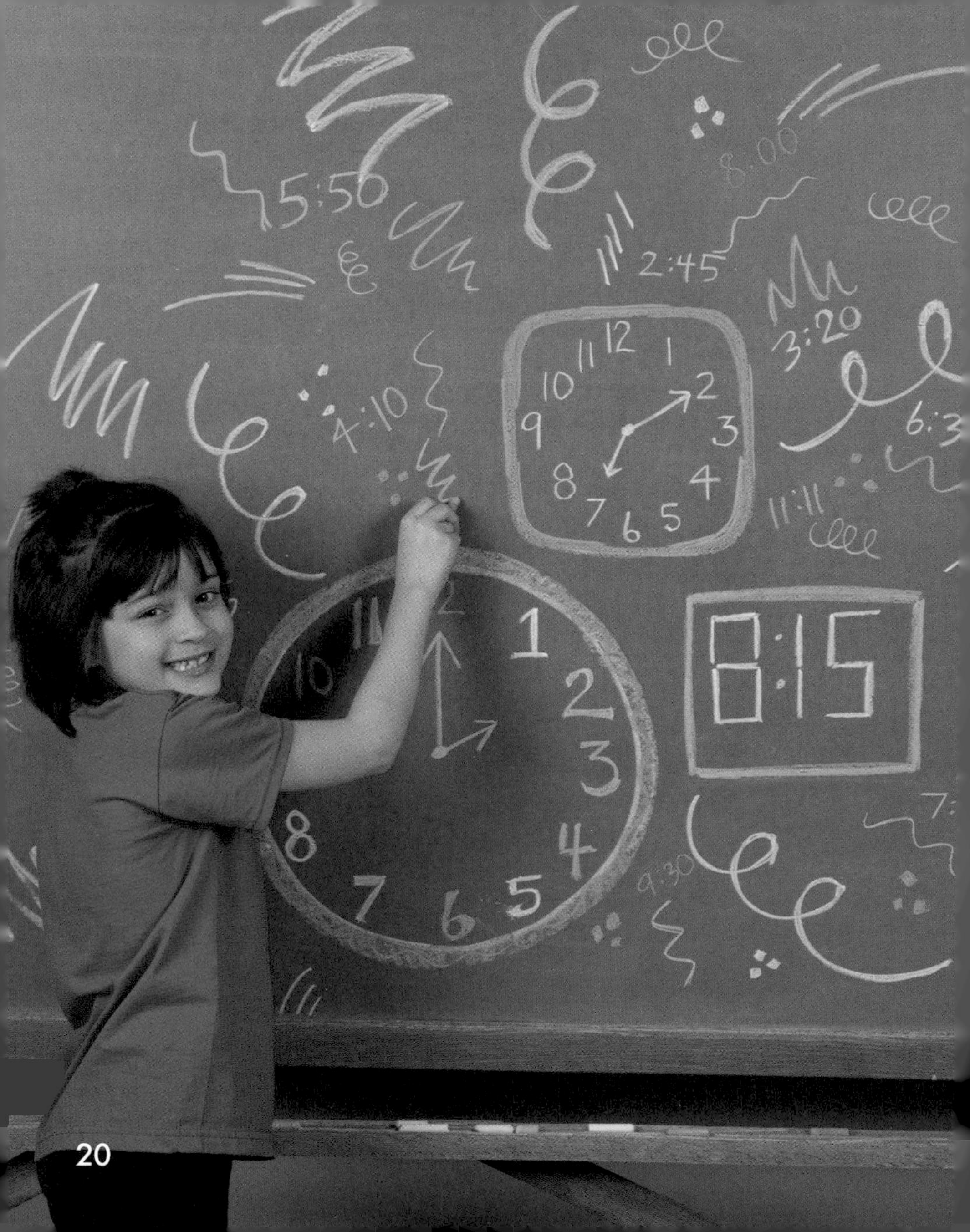
5:50
8:00
2:45
3:20
4:10
11:11
8:15
9:30

That's a minute
on our clock.
Sixty seconds—
tickety tock!

Glossary

bait—to use a small amount of food to get an animal to come near or to bite a hook

clock—something used to measure and show time

face—the front side of a clock; it shows the numbers and hands of the clock

hand—a pointer on a clock

jot—to write quickly or in a hurry

minute—a unit of time that is equal to 60 seconds

second—a unit of time that is one of 60 equal parts of a minute

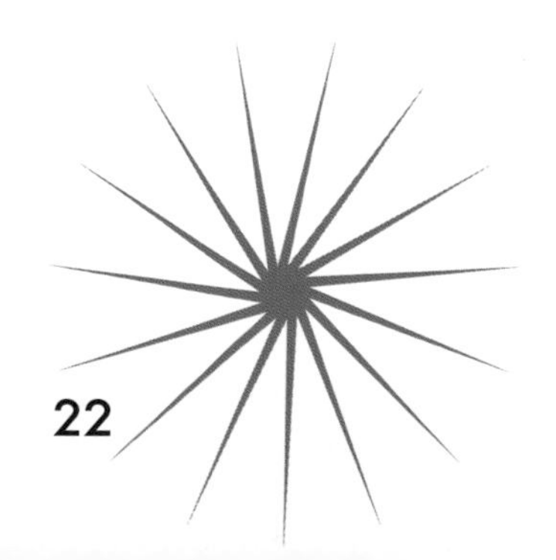

Read More

Gleick, Beth. *Time Is When.* Plattsburgh, N.Y.: Tundra Books, 2008.

Harris, Trudy. *The Clock Struck One: A Time-Telling Tale.* Minneapolis: Millbrook Press, 2009.

Steffora, Tracey. *Hours, Minutes, and Seconds.* Measuring Time. Chicago: Heinemann Library, 2011.

Internet Sites

FactHound offers a safe, fun way to find Internet sites related to this book. All of the sites on FactHound have been researched by our staff.

Here's all you do:

Visit *www.facthound.com*

Type in this code: 9781429685764

Check out projects, games and lots more at
www.capstonekids.com

Index

Word Count: 148
Grade: 1
Early-Intervention Level: 16

Editorial Credits
Gillia Olson, editor; Lori Bye, designer; Sarah Schuette, photo stylist; Marcy Morin, studio scheduler; Kathy McColley, production specialist

Photo Credits
All photos by Capstone Studio/Karon Dubke

J 529.2 HUTMACHER
Hutmacher, Kimberly
Minutes

R0119751415 MECHVL

AUG 0 7 2012

MECHANICSVILLE
Atlanta-Fulton Public Library